AFTERNOON TEA

PHOTOGRAPHY AND DESIGN
BY KOREN TRYGG
TEXT BY LUCY POSHEK

ANTIOCH GOURMET
GIFT BOOKS

Published by Antioch Publishing Company
Yellow Springs, Ohio 45387

ISBN 0-89954-830-X

AFTERNOON TEA

Printed and bound in the U.S.A.

Contents

A History of Tea Drinking

For most of us, afternoon tea evokes classic scenes of British gentility: velvet-draped parlors and orderly gardens; little tables covered with delicate lace, porcelain tea cups, and a scrumptious array of sweets. That magic hour of four o'clock when, not so long ago, the whole of Britain came to a welcome halt.

The British turned afternoon tea into a ritual literally steeped in national identity. But tea drinking itself had already been popularized by other cultures long before it was introduced to Britain.

Legend has it that tea—originally called *cha*—was first discovered four thousand years ago when, by happy accident, some tea leaves blew into the Chinese emperor's kettle of boiling water. Believing the drink had medicinal virtues, the Chinese began consuming tea on a daily basis.

The Japanese first emphasized the aesthetics of the tea-serving ritual. Along with their tea houses and tea gardens, they developed a full set of formal rules governing the brewing and serving of the drink.

Tea was introduced to Russia and Western Europe in the early 1600's. As it was wildly expensive to import from China, the drink grew into a status symbol among the aristocracy. It was not until the nineteenth century, when fast clipper ships and new tea plantations in India were

established, that tea became affordable to all classes of society.

The notion of serving food with afternoon tea developed in the 1700's and is often credited to Anna, the Duchess of Bedford. By then it was the custom to have a large breakfast, light lunch, and late dinner, which left many people waning by late afternoon. To tide her guests over between meals, the duchess began serving tea and light refreshments at four o'clock. Before long it became quite the fashion for ladies to invite friends to the drawing rooms of their homes for afternoon tea.

By the Victorian era, a woman was judged for her social graces largely by the manner in which her afternoon tea was served. Sitting primly behind an ornate silver service, the hostess poured tea into delicate, nearly transparent porcelain cups. Trays of dainty sandwiches, cakes, and sweets were served with white, lace-trimmed napkins. Conversation was light and solicitous: "One lump or two? Milk or lemon?"

These days, afternoon tea can be anything from a brief, solitary break with a mug and a snack to an elaborate, formal buffet. Whatever the presentation, the purpose of afternoon tea is much the same as it was in earlier times: to calm the mind and retreat for a few moments from the pressures of the outside world; to refresh oneself and one's friends with a bit of momentary pleasure. Afternoon tea is not a meal so much as an experience—a step back in time to a gentler era.

A Word About High Tea

Many people think high tea is a more elaborate version of low tea, or afternoon tea. But high tea was originally the evening meal for Victorian working classes. A sit-down supper, it usually consisted of heavier dishes such as Welsh rarebit, treacle, plum pudding, kippers, breads, and cakes. Although accompanied by pints of strong tea (or ale, more likely), the assembly of hearty foods makes it distinctly different from the delicate fare of afternoon tea.

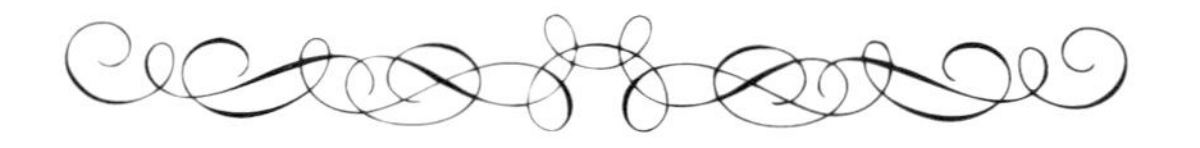

"In nothing more is the English genius for domesticity more notably declared than in the institution of this festival—almost one may call it—of afternoon tea...The mere chink of cups and saucers tunes the mind to happy repose."

George Gissing

TYPES OF TEA

Tea is an evergreen tropical bush that, like coffee, produces leaves after the first five years. The gathering of the green leaves is done by hand over a six-month period. The first "flush" leaves or "pluckings" of the season are best. After the green leaves are "withered" in dry, warm air, they are then "rolled" to release unwanted moisture.

The leaf can remain fresh as *green tea*, or be partially fermented into copper-colored *oolong* tea, or fully fermented and fired in ovens, which produces *black* tea.

Green tea is light and clear with a delicate flavor and the least amount of caffeine. Oolong tea is rich and fruity. Black tea, the strongest, accounts for most of the tea consumed in the United States.

The taste of tea also depends on where it was grown, the climate, manufacturing process, leaf size, and whether the tea is scented, flavored, or blended. Most tea drunk today is blended.

Traditionally, the oolong and more delicate black teas have been favored for afternoon tea. Strong teas such as Keemun and English Breakfast are best with full meals or as morning eye-openers because of their robust flavor and higher caffeine content. Whatever the strength of the tea, consider how the flavor will complement the type of food you are serving. A smoky tea, for example, will be a better match with savory foods than with sweets.

Herbal teas are not true teas, but rather *tisanes*, a mixture of herbs and flowers. Spiced teas consist of spices and fruit peels such as orange, cloves, and cinnamon. Flavored teas usually have only the oils or scents of flavors sprayed on the tea leaves. While many flavored types such as Earl Grey are excellent, the varieties of flavored teas are endless and their quality uncertain.

Ceylon—Grown in the high altitudes of Sri Lanka. Rich flavor, golden color, and fine fragrance. Good served iced with lemon slices.

Darjeeling—Fine tea from the Himalayas. Delicate flavor, amber color. One of the most costly Indian teas, usually reserved for special occasions. Good unblended.

Earl Grey—A delicate blend of China and Darjeeling teas scented with oil of bergamot. Although originally named after Charles, the second Earl Grey, the tea was never patented, so many merchants now use its name. Light, sweet, citrusy flavor. An afternoon tea favorite. Goes well with sweets. Serve with a slice of lemon or bit of milk.

Jasmine—Beautifully scented, semifermented tea. Exotic, light flavor. Should be drunk plain or with a slice of lemon. Contains dried jasmine blossoms among the leaves.

Keemun—From China and Taiwan, this black tea has a strong, rich taste. Serve with milk but no sugar. Good with heartier food.

Lapsang Souchong—Distinctively smoky flavor and aroma. May need an acquired taste. Complements savory foods such as tea sandwiches. Best outdoors tea. Usually taken with lemon or alone.

Formosa Oolong—From China. Subtle, fruity flavor and bouquet. Goes well with light foods and desserts. Among the finest of teas. Other oolongs also make good afternoon teas.

Orange Pekoe—This is a grade of black tea rather than a blend. Orange refers to the color of the leaf, not the flavor, while pekoe (pronounced PEE-ko) refers to leaf size—the largest grade of leaf—only. Makes one of the finest, sweetest cups of afternoon tea.

Yunnan—Light, delicate tea from Western China. Golden color and slightly malty taste.

ABCDEF

THE PERFECT POT OF TEA

Although a fine quality of fresh tea leaves certainly helps, the brewing method is really the key to a good, rich cup of tea. Here's how:

—Begin with fresh, cold water.

—Use a ceramic teapot—it retains heat and flavor best.

—Warm the teapot first by rinsing with hot water.

—Measure one heaping teaspoon of tea per cup plus one for the pot. If using tea bags, count on one bag for each tea cup (about six ounces).

—Do not let the water overboil. Remove the tea kettle when it has reached the just-boiling point and pour the water immediately into the teapot.

—Cover the pot with a lid and brew the tea for three to five minutes before pouring. The larger the tea leaves the longer the brewing time. Brew by the time, not the color, and no more than five minutes.

—Remove the tea leaves or bags from the brewed tea to keep it from getting bitter. Use a tea ball or strain the tea into a second warmed pot. A tea cozy will help keep the pot warm.

—Stir the tea before pouring. If taking milk, add it to the cup first. Cold, whole milk is preferable over cream. Never add milk to green or oolong teas. Add sweeteners, if desired, and then lemon.

TEA ACCESSORIES

In the eighteenth century, elegant silver tea services were a status symbol in England. The costly tea leaves were packed in small canister boxes called tea caddies and were usually kept under lock and key. A caddy spoon, mote spoon (designed for straining tea leaves from the poured tea and cleaning the spout of the teapot), tea strainer, tea kettle, pot, sugar canister, tongs, spoon tray, milk and cream jugs were all brought in on a silver tray. Tea cups, saucers, and spoons were set on a separate tea table. Buns or scones were presented in silver muffin dishes with domed lids; later, three-tiered cake stands came along. Then there were lemon forks, sandwich servers, butter picks, sauce ladles...the list goes on. In fact, by the late 1800's, some silver manufacturers offered as many as 250 tea accessories within one pattern.

Although elaborate tea services are rarely used now, the enjoyment of the ritual is still enhanced by a lovely presentation. In addition to a china or pottery teapot (most purists agree that silver can distort the taste of tea), cups and saucers, the following accessories will help.

Unless using tea bags, a tea infuser or tea ball will prevent the tea leaves from floating around in the pot or straying into the cups. This perforated hollow container is removed after the brewing process. When tea is brewed

TEA

with loose leaves, a tea strainer comes in handy—placed over the teacup, it catches the leaves when the tea is poured.

Tea cozies are used often in Britain, and they really do help keep the teapot warm. Usually made from quilted fabric, some tea cozies allow the handle and spout to poke out; others fit over the entire pot and must be removed to pour the tea.

As with the serving of coffee, a milk pitcher and sugar bowl are standard items on the tea table. Sugar cubes are becoming more obsolete, but when using them, a pair of sugar tongs makes an elegant accompaniment. (And this affords you the chance to ask, "One lump, or two?") Otherwise, use a sugar spoon. If serving lemon slices with tea, a little lemon fork is also handy.

Tea cups and plates do not, by any means, need to match. Collecting individual cups is now a common practice, and afternoon tea provides the perfect occasion to show them off. Pretty linens—dainty napkins and a tablecloth—make the experience of afternoon tea even more special.

"There is a great deal of poetry and fine sentiment in a chest of tea."

RALPH WALDO EMERSON

Cream Tea

There is perhaps nothing more warming to the soul than hot scones spread generously with sweet jam and clotted cream, along with a hearty cup of tea. When tea is accompanied by scones, jam, and cream, this is called a cream tea.

Cream teas are a luscious specialty of Devonshire and Cornwall, England, where real clotted cream is served. Unpasteurized creamy milk is scalded, then left to stand for twenty-four hours in a cool place. A thick yellow crust—the clotted part—forms on the top of the pan. Since clotted cream is hard to find and make in the United States, most American tea shops simply serve whipped cream instead. But if you ever get a chance to taste real clotted cream, it is an experience not to be missed.

Menu

Raisin Scones
Mock Devonshire Cream
Strawberry Jam
Orange Pekoe or Earl Grey Tea

Raisin Scones

2 cups (16 fl. oz.) flour
1 tbsp. (3/4 Br. tbsp.) baking powder
2 tbsp. (1 1/2 Br. tbsp.) sugar
1/2 tsp. salt
4 tbsp. (3 Br. tbsp.) butter
5 1/2 tbsp. (4 Br. tbsp.) cream
2 eggs, beaten, with part of the whites reserved
1/2 cup (4 fl. oz.) raisins

Preheat oven to 400°F. Sift flour, baking powder, sugar, and salt into a bowl. Cut in butter until mixture is fine and crumbly. Combine cream with eggs and add to flour mixture to make stiff dough; also add raisins. Knead gently on a lightly floured surface until dough is sticky. Divide in half; roll out each half into a 6-inch circle about 1 inch thick. Cut circles into quarters. Place on ungreased baking sheet about one inch apart. Brush tops with reserved egg white; dust with sugar. Bake for 10 to 15 minutes or until golden brown. Makes 8 scones.

Mock Devonshire Cream

1/2 cup (4 fl. oz.) whipping cream
1/2 cup (4 fl. oz.) sour cream
1 tsp. (3/4 Br. tsp.) powdered (icing) sugar (opt.)

Beat cream in chilled bowl until stiff. Add sugar and fold in sour cream. Serve over scones with jam. Makes 1 1/2 cups (12 fl. oz.).

FORMAL VICTORIAN TEA

Victorian teas are the most traditional and elegant of afternoon teas. During Queen Victoria's reign in the 1800's, afternoon tea consisted of dainty little sandwiches filled with thin cucumbers or potted meat; fancy, dry biscuits (dry so guests wouldn't soil their fingers) such as shortbread, and various cakes. They were presented on delicate bone china with silver accessories and all the proper decorum fitting to the century.

The teatime sandwich (said to have been invented by the Earl of Sandwich in the eighteenth century) is meant to be a tasty tidbit and savory counterpoint to the sweet offerings. Endless variations are possible with different combinations of spreads, breads, fillings, and garnishes. Parsley, watercress, chives, caviar, sliced strawberries, tomatoes, and stuffed olives all make good garnishes.

MENU

Cucumber Sandwiches
Shortbread
Chocolate Rum Torte
Poppy Seed Cake
Darjeeling or Formosa Oolong Tea

Cucumber Sandwiches

1 large hothouse or English cucumber
1 tbsp. (3/4 Br. tbsp.) white wine vinegar
salt and white pepper to taste
1 small bunch red radishes
unsalted butter or cream cheese
thinly sliced bread
watercress (opt.)

Slice cucumber very thinly; sprinkle slices with vinegar and salt and white pepper to taste. Let stand for several hours. Wash, trim and slice radishes crosswise.

Spread butter on thin slices of bread. Then trim the crusts and cut each slice into 4 squares or triangles. Drain cucumber slices; pat dry with paper towels. Layer cucumber slices on buttered bread and overlap with radish slices. If desired, garnish with watercress.

A Word About Tea Sandwiches

Although tea sandwiches are no longer restricted to white bread, the bread should still be untextured, firm, and very thinly sliced. Spreading the bread with softened butter, cream cheese, or herbed mayonnaise will keep it moist and also prevent sogginess. For a neater finish to the edges, it is sometimes better to remove the crusts after the sandwiches have been spread, not before. Then the slices may be quartered and cut into triangles or other shapes with a cookie cutter.

A one-pound loaf of bread yields about thirty small sandwiches. Allow around three sandwiches per person.

Shortbread

½ lb. softened butter
1 tsp. (¾ Br. tsp.) vanilla
2 cups (16 fl. oz.) flour
½ cup (4 fl. oz.) powdered (icing) sugar
¼ cup (2 fl. oz.) granulated sugar

Preheat oven to 325°F. Cream butter and vanilla together in a medium mixing bowl. Sift flour and both sugars into butter mixture and thoroughly blend. Press dough into the bottom of an ungreased 8-inch round cake pan. With a sharp knife, score dough into 8 wedges. Prick dough all over with a fork. Bake for 20 minutes, until shortbread is lightly golden or wooden toothpick placed in center comes out clean. Cut into wedges while hot but leave in pan to cool.

"The tea equipage is usually placed upon a silver-salver or china kettle on a stand and the cups are small. Thin bread and butter, cake, petits-fours and sometimes fresh fruit are all the eatables given. These are daintily arranged on plates, spread with lace doilies, and placed in a cakestand or on a convenient table."

MRS. BEETON
The Book of Household Management

Chocolate Rum Torte

Torte

4 oz. semisweet (or milk) chocolate
2 tbsp. (1½ Br. tbsp.) rum
¼ lb. softened butter
⅔ cup (5⅓ fl. oz.) and 1 tbsp. (¾ Br. tbsp.) sugar
3 eggs, separated
⅓ cup (2⅔ fl. oz.) pulverized almonds
¼ tsp. almond extract
¼ cup (2 fl. oz.) flour

Glaze

1 oz. semisweet (or milk) chocolate
1 tbsp. (¾ Br. tbsp.) rum
3 tbsp. (2¼ Br. tbsp.) butter

Preheat oven to 350°F. Butter and flour an 8-inch round cake pan, placing a round piece of wax paper in the bottom if desired.

Melt the chocolate and rum over hot water. In a separate bowl, cream the butter, ⅔ cup (5⅓ fl. oz.) sugar and egg yolks together. Add the melted chocolate to the butter mixture, then add pulverized almonds and almond extract.

In another bowl, beat the egg whites until soft peaks form. Add 1 tbsp. (¾ Br. tbsp.) sugar and continue beating until fairly stiff. Fold a fourth of the egg whites into the chocolate batter. Then, working

quickly, fold in the remaining egg whites, alternating with the flour. Pour into cake pan.

Bake on the middle rack of the oven for 20 to 25 minutes. Torte is done when a toothpick comes clean from the outside perimeter but slightly oily from the center. Cool on a rack and remove to a flat plate.

Melt the chocolate square and rum over hot water and stir until smooth. Beat in butter a bit at a time. When glaze has cooled, spread over top of torte. Decorate with additional almonds, if desired.

Poppy Seed Cake

3 cups (24 fl. oz.) flour
2½ cups (20 fl. oz.) sugar
1½ tsp. (1 Br. tsp.) salt
1½ tsp. (1 Br. tsp.) baking powder
3 eggs
1½ cups (12 fl. oz.) milk
1½ cups (12 fl. oz.) oil
1½ tbsp. (1 Br. tbsp.) poppy seeds
1½ tsp. (1 Br. tsp.) each vanilla, butter, and almond extract

Preheat oven to 325°F. Mix all ingredients together and pour into a greased and floured bundt pan or 2 loaf pans. Bake for one hour or until toothpick inserted comes out clean.

Garden Tea

What better way to highlight a tea out in the garden or on the patio than with herbs and fruit? If the day is warm, iced tea offers a refreshing alternative to hot tea.

The secret for good iced tea is to brew the tea double or triple strength and chill it in the refrigerator. Garnish the pitcher or tall glasses with fresh mint leaves or lemon slices and serve with plenty of ice. Ceylon, Yunnan, Jasmine, and many herbal teas are good when iced.

If you have several hours, you can make sun tea: Combine the tea leaves or bags with water in a glass jar and set the jar in the sun. When ready to serve, shake the jar and strain the tea into tall glasses.

Menu

Herbed Cheese & Smoked Salmon Sandwiches

Lemon Curd Squares

Fresh Seasonal Fruit

Iced Tea

Herbed Cheese and Smoked Salmon Sandwiches

1 cup (8 fl. oz.) lowfat cottage cheese
2 tsp. (1½ Br. tsp.) skim milk
½ tsp. ground pepper
1 tbsp. (¾ Br. tbsp.) chopped parsley
¼ tsp. thyme
½ clove garlic, peeled
tea sandwich bread
smoked salmon, thinly sliced

Mix cottage cheese, milk, and herbs in blender until smooth. (Some extra milk may be needed.) Spread mixture over thin slices of bread; cut off crusts and cut into squares, triangles or circles. Top each sandwich with a slice of smoked salmon and a garnish such as thin lemon slices, watercress, or dill.

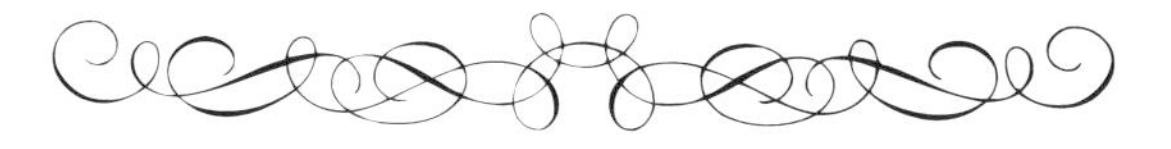

Iced tea was discovered on a hot day in 1904 at the St. Louis World's Fair. Representatives at the Indian tea booth, desperate to entice customers, tried offering their tea poured over ice. People flocked to their booth. Today, most Americans still prefer their tea iced.

Lemon Curd Squares

Crust

½ lb. softened butter
½ cup (4 fl. oz.) powdered (icing) sugar
2 cups (16 fl. oz.) flour
dash of salt

Preheat oven to 350°F. Have ready a 10- x 15-inch jelly roll pan. Blend softened butter with powdered sugar, flour, and salt. Pat evenly into pan; bake for 10 to 15 minutes. Let cool on a rack.

Lemon Curd Filling

3 eggs
5 tbsp. (3¾ Br. tbsp.) melted butter
1 cup (8 fl. oz.) granulated sugar
juice and finely grated outer rind of 2 lemons

Beat eggs into melted butter. Stir in sugar. Beat well. Pour mixture into a double boiler; gradually add lemon juice and rind. Cook until thickened. Pour mixture over the baked crust. Cool thoroughly before cutting into squares.

"Thank God for tea!
What would the world do without tea?–how did it exist? I am glad I was not born before tea."

Sydney Smith

CHILDREN'S TEA

It was once traditional for children to have tea in the nursery with their parents or nanny before bedtime. Called a nursery tea, or children's tea, it was a simple affair consisting of bread or toast and cups of cocoa or cambric tea (milk with a spot of tea).

Children's teas can still be an enjoyable ritual, especially with the attendance of a favorite stuffed bear or two and perhaps a miniature-sized tea set. The "tea" can be milk, lemonade, juice, or cocoa, accompanied by little sandwiches and a sweet. Whatever the setting, the daily or weekly custom of having your children sit down in the afternoon for a nicely presented refreshment will be a heartwarming memory for them later.

MENU

Bread and Butter Sandwiches
Marmalade
Jelly Print Cookies
Ginger Cats
Cambric Tea

Jelly Print Cookies

½ cup (4 fl. oz.) softened butter
¼ cup (2 fl. oz.) packed brown sugar
¼ cup (2 fl. oz.) creamy peanut butter
1 egg, separated
½ tsp. vanilla
1 cup (8 fl. oz.) flour
¼ tsp. salt
¾ cup (6 fl. oz.) finely chopped peanuts
jam or jelly

Preheat oven to 350°F. Cream together the butter, brown sugar, peanut butter, egg yolk, and vanilla. Stir in the flour and salt. Roll into 1-inch balls. Dip them in slightly beaten egg white and then roll in nuts. Place cookies 1 inch apart on ungreased baking sheet. Bake for 5 minutes and remove from oven. Quickly press thumb into the center of each cookie; return to oven and bake 8 minutes longer or until golden brown. Cool. Spoon a bit of jelly into each thumbprint. Makes 2 dozen cookies.

"Christopher Robin was at home by this time...and he was so glad to see them that they stayed there until very nearly tea-time, and then they had a Very Nearly tea, which is one you forget about afterwards..."

The House at Pooh Corner

Ginger Cats

12 tbsp. (9 Br. tbsp.) butter, softened
1 cup (8 fl. oz.) dark brown sugar
1/4 cup (2 fl. oz.) molasses or honey
1 egg
2 1/4 cups (18 fl. oz.) flour
1 tsp. (3/4 Br. tsp.) baking soda
2 tsp. (1 1/2 Br. tsp.) ground ginger
1 tsp. (3/1 Br. tsp.) ground cinnamon
icing (opt.)

Preheat oven to 350°F. Grease cookie sheets. Cream together butter, sugar, egg, and molasses or honey. In a bowl, combine flour, baking soda, ginger, and cinnamon. Stir in butter mixture. Add a little water if necessary to make a firm dough. Roll out onto a lightly-floured board to 1/4-inch thickness. Cut shapes from dough with a cat cookie cutter. Place on baking sheet. Bake for 10 to 15 minutes. Cool on a wire rack. If desired, decorate with icing.
Makes approximately 2 dozen.

"Take some more tea," the March Hare said to Alice very earnestly. "I haven't had any yet," Alice replied in an offended tone, "so I can't take more."

LEWIS CARROLL
Alice in Wonderland

Country Picnic Tea

Whether on the beach or in a park, the outdoors can stimulate a hearty appetite. A picnic tea provides the perfect antidote to those late afternoon rumblings.

Make the tea in advance at home and strain it into a thermos. Add the sugar, milk, or lemon later when serving the tea. Another alternative is to serve iced tea instead.

A country tea needs no fancy accessories. The more rustic, the better. Food can be a bit heartier than when indoors, and the tea should be a robust variety. Prepare dishes that are easy to tote and simple to eat. Bring the picnic in a basket and set the food out on a blanket or country quilt.

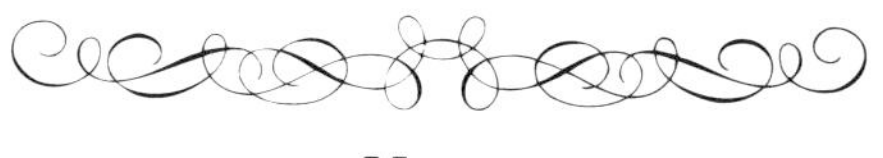

Menu

Indian Chicken Salad
Apple Tartlets
Country Bread
Cheese and Fresh Fruit
Lapsang Souchong or Ceylon Tea

Indian Chicken Salad

Salad

2 cups (16 fl. oz.) cooked chicken, diced
¾ cup (6 fl. oz.) celery, diced
½ cup (4 fl. oz.) shredded coconut

Dressing

½ cup (4 fl. oz.) mayonnaise
½ cup (4 fl. oz.) sour cream
1 tsp. (¾ Br. tsp.) curry powder
1 tsp. (¾ Br. tsp.) lime juice
1 tsp. (¾ Br. tsp.) sugar
1½ tbsp. (1 Br. tbsp.) chutney
pinch of salt and pepper

Mix all ingredients together. Serves 4. (Optional additions: peanuts, raisins, or grapes.)

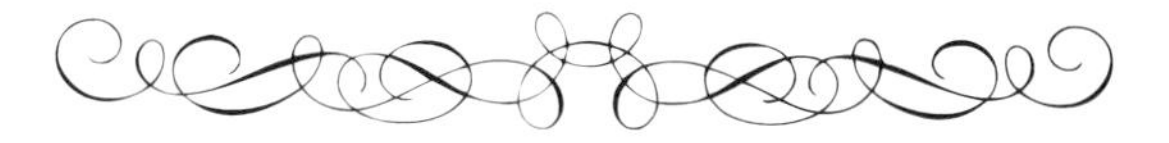

"Tea! Thou soft, thou sober, sage, and venerable liquid, thou female tongue-running, smile-soothing, heart-opening, wink-tippling cordial, to whose glorious insipidity I owe the happiest moments of my life, let me fall prostrate."

COLLEY CIBBER

Apple Tartlets

Tart Shells

½ cup (4 fl. oz.) powdered (icing) sugar
½ lb. unsalted butter, softened
1 tsp. (¾ Br. tsp.) vanilla extract
2 cups (16 fl. oz.) flour
dash of salt
½ cup (4 fl. oz.) blanched almonds, finely chopped

In a large bowl cream together powdered sugar and butter. Add vanilla extract; mix well. Work in flour, salt, and chopped almonds. When dough is smooth, shape it into a ball and wrap it in waxed paper. Chill for 1 hour or more until ready to bake.

Apple Filling

6 Granny Smith apples, cored, peeled and chopped fine
1 tbsp. (¾ Br. tbsp.) water
1 tbsp. (¾ Br. tbsp.) lemon juice
1 tsp. (¾ Br. tsp.) vanilla
1 tsp. (¾ Br. tsp.) cinnamon
1 tsp. (¾ Br. tsp.) sugar
¼ tsp. ground cloves

In a bowl, mix all ingredients together.

Preheat oven to 325°F. Grease tartlet molds or muffin pans. Press dough into each mold until it is evenly and thinly distributed. Fill each shell with apple mixture. Bake for 25 minutes or until golden brown.

HOLIDAY TEA

A warming pot of tea couldn't be more welcome than when the frosty winter holidays are upon us. Traditional English sweets—especially trifle—and spiced cakes, along with savory tidbits, are a natural choice for a merry holiday tea. Sherry or port served in a decanter can be a nice complement to the menu. Set a glittering table or sideboard with your finest dishes surrounded by pine boughs and sparkling ornaments. Add candles and a little classical music to enhance the elegantly festive mood.

Trifle developed from a simple Elizabethan recipe for sugared cream into a colorful, elaborate dessert as more ingredients were added with each passing century. Today's trifle—the layering of cake soaked in brandy with preserves, fruit, custard and whipped cream—creates a wonderfully decadent dish befitting the holidays.

MENU

Spinach Cheese Flan
Cranberry Cream Cheese Bread
Raspberry-Brandy Trifle
Florentines
Keemun, Earl Grey, or Spiced Tea

Spinach Cheese Flan

9-inch unbaked pie shell
1 egg white
1 cup (8 fl. oz.) each Gruyère and fontina cheese, grated
1 tbsp. (3/4 Br. tbsp.) butter or margarine
1 cup (8 fl. oz.) fresh mushrooms, sliced
1 tbsp. (3/4 Br. tbsp.) vegetable oil
1 lb. fresh spinach leaves chopped
3 eggs, slightly beaten
1 1/2 cups (12 fl. oz.) half and half (half cream, half whole milk)
1/4 tsp. nutmeg
1/4 tsp. salt
1/8 tsp. cayenne pepper
1 Roma tomato, seeded and diced

Preheat oven to 450°F. Place unbaked pie shell in a 9-inch quiche or pie pan. Prick sides and bottom of shell. Brush with egg white. Bake for 5 minutes.

Spread cheeses in partially baked pie shell. Sauté mushrooms in butter over medium heat for 1 minute. Drain well. Sauté spinach in oil over medium heat until it starts to wilt. Remove from heat. Place in sieve and press out excess liquid. Layer mushrooms and spinach on top of cheeses.

Mix the eggs with the half and half, nutmeg, salt, and cayenne pepper. Pour egg mixture over cheese and vegetables. Place diced tomatoes on top of filling. Bake 15 minutes at 450°F. Reduce heat to 350°F and cook 10 to 15 minutes longer until filling sets. Serves 6.

Cranberry Cream Cheese Bread

2 cups (16 fl. oz.) flour
3/4 cup (6 fl. oz.) sugar
1 1/2 tsp. (1 Br. tsp.) baking powder
1/2 tsp. baking soda
1 3-oz. package cream cheese
2 tsp. (1 1/2 Br. tsp.) lemon juice
2 tsp. (1 1/2 Br. tsp.) vanilla
2 eggs
1/4 cup (2 fl. oz.) hot melted butter
1/2 cup (4 fl. oz) milk
1 cup (8 fl. oz.) cranberries, fresh or frozen

Preheat oven to 350°F. Combine dry ingredients in bowl. In blender or food processor, blend wet ingredients, in order as listed, until smooth. Pour mixture into bowl with dry ingredients and stir together. Fold in cranberries. Bake in greased bundt cake pan or medium-sized loaf pan for about 1 hour or until toothpick comes out clean from center.

Raspberry-Brandy Trifle

Custard

3 cups (24 fl. oz.) milk
4 tbsp. (3 Br. tbsp.) cornstarch
2 tbsp. (1 1/2 Br. tbsp.) sugar
2 egg yolks
1 tsp. (3/4 Br. tsp.) vanilla

Over medium heat in a heavy 2-quart saucepan, mix 1/2 cup (4 fl. oz.) milk and the cornstarch. Add remaining milk and sugar, and stir constantly until it thickens

and comes to a boil. Remove from heat.

In a small bowl beat eggs and a small amount of the custard mixture with a fork. Return to saucepan. Bring to a boil again. Boil 1 minute, stirring constantly. Remove from heat and add vanilla.

Note: You may prepare the custard and cake in advance and refrigerate until ready to assemble the trifle.

Trifle

1 12-oz. pound cake mix, baked according to directions
4 tbsp. (3 Br. tbsp.) good quality raspberry jam
1 cup (8 fl. oz.) slivered blanched almonds
1 cup (8 fl. oz.) medium dry drinking sherry
¼ cup (2 fl. oz.) brandy
2 cups (16 fl. oz.) heavy cream
2 tbsp. (1½ Br. tbsp.) sugar
2 cups (16 fl. oz.) fresh raspberries

Cut two or three 1-inch thick slices of the cake and coat them with jam. Place slices in the bottom of a large glass bowl, jam side up. Cut remaining cake into 1-inch cubes and scatter them over the slices. On top of the cake sprinkle a half-cup of the almonds, then the sherry and brandy; let stand for 30 minutes.

Whip the cream, add sugar, then whip again until stiff. Set aside ten of the best-looking berries and pour the rest over the cake. Spread custard over the berries with a spatula. Add whipped cream last, and top with remaining berries and almonds.

Florentines

5 tbsp. (3¾ Br. tbsp.) butter
½ cup (4 fl. oz.) light brown sugar
3 tbsp. (2¼ Br. tbsp.) heavy cream
¾ cup (6 fl. oz.) almonds, finely chopped
2 tbsp. (1½ Br. tbsp.) candied cherries, finely chopped
¼ cup (2 fl. oz.) shredded coconut
4 oz. melted chocolate (opt.)

Preheat oven to 350°F. Grease 2 cookie sheets. In a medium pan over medium heat, melt butter. Add the sugar and cook for 2 minutes. Stir in the cream, almonds, candied cherries, and coconut; remove from heat. Drop 5 to 6 heaping teaspoons onto each cookie sheet, allowing room for them to spread. Bake 8 to 10 minutes. Remove from oven. Let set on cookie sheets for 5 minutes, then carefully transfer cookies to wire rack to cool. Drizzle with melted chocolate, if desired. Makes 12 cookies.

"Surely everyone is aware of the divine pleasures which attend a wintry fireside: candles at four o'clock, warm hearth rugs, tea, a fair tea-maker, shutters closed, curtains flowing in ample draperies to the floor, whilst the wind and rain are raging audibly without."
THOMAS DE QUINCEY

"If you are cold, tea will warm you–if you are too heated, it will cool you–if you are depressed, it will cheer you–if you are excited, it will calm you."

William Gladstone

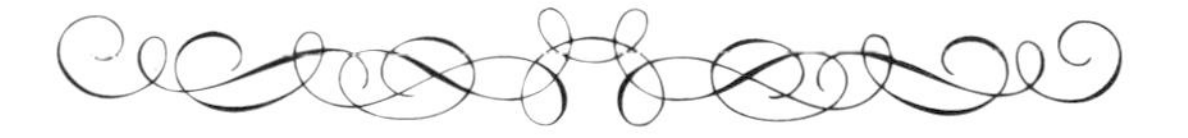

Graphic Design by Gretchen Goldie

Photo Styling and Sets by Sue Tallon

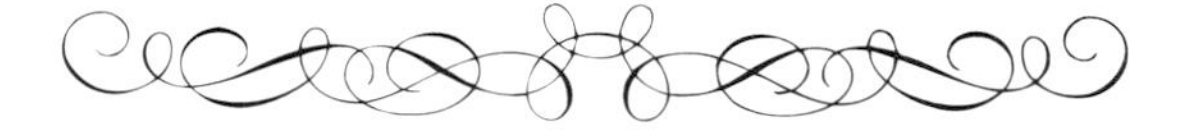

Acknowledgments

Pamela Barrus, Anita Buchanan, Eleanor Christensen, Hilary Cohen, Becky Habblett, Ruth Hanks, Jean Hyde, Deborah Joyce, Hilde Linke, Susan Maljan, Debra Nessel, Christine Tallon, Juliette Trygg